CELLO

Duets for Strings

BY
SAMUEL APPLEBAUM

MW00666932

FOREWORD

The Duets For Strings Book II may be started when the pupil has reached Page 5 of Volume II of the String Builder. They may, however, be used in conjunction with Volume II of any standard string class Method. These Duets may be played by:

Two Violins	Violin and Viola	Viola and Cello	Cello and Bass
Two Violas	Violin and Cello	Viola and Bass	
Two Cellos	Violin and Bass		
Two Basses			

The Duets in this book are in the major keys of C, G, F, D and B♭ in that order. The bowings used are the Détaché and the Martelé in various parts of the bow. The first position is used for all the string instruments, except the Bass. In the flat keys, the Bass uses the half position.

The two slanted lines (//) mean that the bow is to be lifted from the string. This is done usually at the end of a phrase. Its purpose is to make the pupil cognizant of the architecture of each duet by pointing out the phrases. Lifting and re-setting the bow helps to develop control of the bow arm.

The comma (⟩) means a slight pause, also usually at the end of a phrase, with the bow remaining on the string. This usually occurs when the phrase ends on the down bow above the middle of the bow.

These duets are carefully chosen and arranged to provide technical benefit and musical enjoyment. They are particularly useful for school recitals. Each duet may be played twice with the partners changing parts.

Contents

2

1. The two slanted lines (//) mean that you are to lift the bow from the string.
2. Leave a slight pause at each comma (𝄒) with the bow remaining on the string.

1. March

C. HOHMANN

2. Passepied

G. F. HANDEL

These duets are in the Key of G Major. The name of the sharp is F. Every F is to be raised.

3. Russian Folk Song

L. VAN BEETHOVEN

4. Menuett

G. F. HANDEL

4

1. These duets are in the Key of F Major. The name of the flat is B. The B flats are played with the 2nd finger on G and the 1st finger on the A string.

2. A Sarabande is a dignified dance of Spanish or Oriental origin in 3/4 time.

3. A Gavotte is a lively old French dance usually in 4/4 time beginning on an up-beat.

5. Sarabande

J. KUHNAU

6. Gavotte

G. F. HANDEL

gradually softer   *p*   *gradually louder*

Repeat this duet changing parts.

1. Notice the dotted quarter notes. Be sure to hold them for their full value.

2. In Duet No. 8, (10th and 13th measures – lower line) we have C♯ on the G string. Practice these measures a few times making sure that the C♯ is in tune.

7. Menuett

JOHANN J. FUX

8. Gavotte

G. F. HANDEL

In the 17th measure (lower line) we have another C♯ on the G string.

9. Flower Waltz

JOSEPH REINAGLE

In No. 10 listen carefully to the quarter notes. In No. 11 listen carefully to the eighth notes. They must move together.

10. Sarabande

DANIEL SPEER

11. Evening Song

W. A. MOZART

A Bourrée is a lively dance of French or Spanish origin beginning with an up-beat. It is usually in 4/4 or 2/4 time.

12. Bourrée

J. S. BACH

13. Hallelujah

ROUND IN TWO PARTS

1. A Pavane is a stately dance of Italian or Spanish origin in 4/4 time.

2. A Canon is musical imitation very much like the Rounds that you sing in school.

14. Pavane

Allegretto (Key of F)

PAUL PEUERL

15. Canon

Moderato (Key of G)

KUNRAD KUNZ

In No. 16 listen carefully to the eighth notes. They must move together.

16. Air

Listen carefully to the quarter notes and the eighth notes when both parts move together.

18. Passepied

G. P. TELEMANN

19. Canon

KUNRAD KUNZ

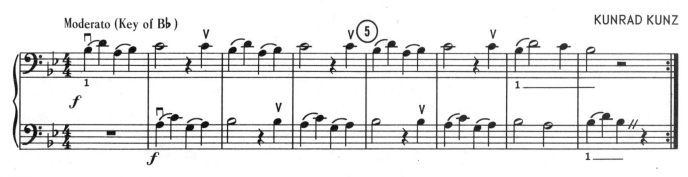

Notice the extended position. Practice these passages separately. Make sure that the left thumb is always behind or opposite the 2nd finger.

20. Sarabande

21. The Rhyme

22. Flight

Use the Martelé bowing on the notes marked with dots. Leave a clean stop between each martelé note.
Please observe the accent marks using more bow on these notes.

23. A Rondo Theme

I. PLEYEL

24. Quiet Motion

17TH CENTURY CANON

Use about three inches of bow for the martelé notes when playing "piano". In the "forte" passages use most of the bow for the martelé notes.

25. Le Petit Rien

FRANCOIS COUPERIN

26. A Gentle Breeze

17TH CENTURY CANON

1. In measures 4, 8, 12, 16, 20 and 24 of Duet No. 28, play the last note of the measure softly, as it ends the phrase.

2. Review your favorite duets in this book changing parts with your partner.

27. The Bluebird

28. Minuet